To:

_____

From:

_____

Editing by: Alice Patenaude
Cover and internal design by: Brian Frantz

Photo Credits
Cover: Khoroshunova Olga/Shutterstock
Internals: pages 2-3, ANP/Shutterstock; page 6, kwest/Shutterstock; page 12, Andrey tiyk/Shutterstock;
page 18, Krivosheev Vitaly/Shutterstock; page 24, Subbotina Anna/Shutterstock; page 30, elementals/
Shutterstock; page 36: Verkhovynets Taras/Shutterstock; page 42, Hemera/Thinkstock; page 48, iStock/
Thinkstock; page 54, John Wollwerth/Shutterstock; page 60, isarescheewin/Shutterstock; page
66, Standret/Shutterstock; page 72, Viviana74GV/Shutterstock; page 84, Creative Travel Projects/
Shutterstock; pages 90 and 96, Tomas1111/Shutterstock; pages 102 and 108, beerlogoff/Shutterstock

Published by Simple Truths, an imprint of Sourcebooks, Inc.
P.O. Box 4410, Naperville, Illinois 60567-4410
(630) 961-3900 • Fax: (630) 961-2168
www.sourcebooks.com

Printed and bound in the United States of America

WOZ 10 9 8 7 6 5 4 3 2 1

STEPHEN R. COVEY

Great Quotes on

LEADERSHIP
and LIFE

simple truths®
Your Destination For Inspiration

an imprint of Sourcebooks, Inc.

Introduction

"The key to life is not accumulation. It's contribution."

That quote from Stephen R. Covey described how he lived his own life. He was a legendary figure—an internationally respected leadership authority, family expert, teacher, organizational consultant and author, whose advice gave insight to millions.

As a teenager, a promising athletic career for Stephen was cut short by degeneration in his legs that caused him to use crutches for three years. After serving in Britain as a missionary for his faith, he decided not to enter the family hotel business, but instead dedicated his passion, ability, skills, and leadership to teaching.

He more than fulfilled that role, in venues from the classroom to the boardroom. In 1996, Stephen was recognized as one of *TIME* magazine's 25 Most Influential Americans. He is the author of more than a dozen books, but the book which was most influential in the lives of millions was the international bestseller, *The 7 Habits of Highly Effective People*. That book sold more than 20 million copies and was named one of the most influential books of the 20th century.

In 1983, he made the decision to leave full-time teaching as a university professor at Brigham Young University to establish the Covey Leadership Center, a training and consulting firm. The Covey Leadership Center later merged with Franklin Quest to form Franklin Covey Co., a global performance improvement company that now operates in 147 countries throughout the world.

From elementary school students to Fortune 100 CEOs and numerous heads of state, Stephen made teaching principle-centered leadership his life's work. The world lost this extraordinary treasure in 2012 at age 79, when he died as a result of complications from a bicycle accident.

I will miss the unique contribution that Stephen brought to the world, but we are lucky to have his writing and his inspiration from which we can draw. Stephen's personal motto was to "live life in crescendo." He felt a persistent desire to stretch himself in new directions, drawing upon the wisdom of respected leaders around the world.

In Stephen R. Covey's *Great Quotes on Leadership and Life*, I'm pleased to share with you many of the quotes from Stephen's books which he found personally inspiring.

As Stephen said in his book, *Everyday Greatness*, "My desire is that some piece of what you read will provide the nudge you may be seeking to advance you from doing good to doing your best, both today and in your pathways ahead!"

Enjoy the wisdom from the ages that inspired one of the great men of our age.

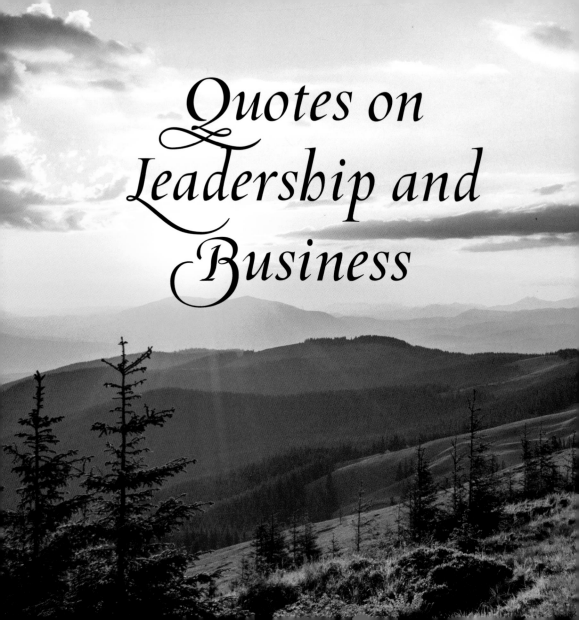

Quotes on Leadership and Business

So much of what we call management consists in making it difficult for people to work.

———————

Peter Drucker

Leadership is the capacity to translate vision into reality.

———————

Warren Bennis

All organizations are perfectly aligned
to get the results they get.

———————

Arthur W. Jones

The very essence of leadership is that you have to have vision. You can't blow an uncertain trumpet.

———————

Theodore W. Hesburgh

The best way to inspire people to superior performance is to convince them by everything you do and by your everyday attitude that you are wholeheartedly supporting them.

———————

Harold S. Geneen

We must sail sometimes with the wind and sometimes against it, but we must sail, and not drift, nor lie at anchor.

Oliver Wendell Holmes Sr.

*O*pportunities are usually disguised as hard work,
so most people don't recognize them.

———————

Ann Landers

A sensible man never embarks on
an enterprise until he can see his way
clear to the end of it.

———

Aesop

*H*appiness, wealth, and success are by-products
of goal setting; they cannot be the goal themselves.

———

Denis Waitley

The majority of hiring mistakes made every day would be prevented if the people responsible for the hiring simply did a more effective job of determining exactly what they were looking for before they started to look.

———————

Robert Half

Plans are worthless; but planning is invaluable.

Peter Drucker

The beginning is the most important part of any work.

Plato

You see things; and you say, "Why?"

But I dream things that never were

and say, "Why not?"

———————

George Bernard Shaw

I know of no more encouraging fact than the unquestionable ability of man to elevate his life by conscious endeavor.

———————

Henry David Thoreau

Failing to plan is a plan to fail.

Effie Jones

I have learned that success is to be measured not so much by the position that one has reached in life as by the obstacles which he has overcome while trying to succeed.

———

Booker T. Washington

*T*here is only one big risk you should avoid at all costs and that is the risk of doing nothing.

———

Denis Waitley

*T*o accomplish great things, we must not only
act, but also dream; not only plan, but also believe.

———————

Anatole France

*Y*ou can't build a reputation
on what you are going to do.

———————

Henry Ford

There is no such thing as *can't*, only *won't*.
If you're qualified, all it takes is a burning
desire to accomplish, to make a change.

———

Jan Ashford

Leaders do not avoid, repress, or deny
conflict, but rather see it as an opportunity.

———

Warren Bennis

If you don't know where you are going, you will probably end up somewhere else.

Laurence J. Peter

Far and away the best prize life has to offer is the chance to work hard at work worth doing.

Theodore Roosevelt

Fixing your objective is like identifying the North Star—you sight your company on it and then use it as a means of getting back on track when you tend to stray.

———

Marshall E. Dimock

Problems are only opportunities in work clothes.

———

Henry J. Kaiser

If one advances confidently in the direction
of his dreams, and endeavors to live the life
which he has imagined, he will meet with a
success unexpected in common hours.

———————

Henry David Thoreau

The secret of success is constancy to purpose.

———————

Benjamin Disraeli

The great thing in this world is not so much where we stand

as in what direction we are moving.

———————

Oliver Wendell Holmes Sr.

Never promise more than you can perform.

Publilius Syrus

Let us never negotiate out of fear.
But let us never fear to negotiate.

John F. Kennedy

Work expands so as to fill time available for its completion.

———

Cyril Northcote Parkinson

It seems rather incongruous that in a society of supersophisticated communication, we often suffer from a shortage of listeners.

———

Erma Bombeck

Discovery consists of seeing what everybody has seen and thinking what nobody has thought.

Albert Szent-Györgi

Never impose your language on people you wish to reach.

———————

Abbie Hoffman

One of the best ways to persuade others is with your ears—by listening to them.

———————

Dean Rusk

If two men on the same job agree all the time, then one is useless.

If they disagree all the time, then both are useless.

———————

Darryl F. Zanuck

The significant problems we face cannot be solved at the

same level of thinking we were at when we created them.

———————

Albert Einstein

*O*ver the years, many executives have said
to me with pride, "Boy, I worked so hard last
year that I didn't take any vacation." I always
feel like responding, "You dummy. You mean to
tell me that you can take responsibility for an
eighty-million-dollar project and you can't plan
two weeks out of the year to have some fun?"

———————

Lee Iacocca

Some can't distinguish between being busy and being productive. They are human windmills, flailing at work, but actually accomplishing little.

———————

Caroline Donnelly, *Money*

My advice to salesmen is this: pretend that every single person you meet has a sign around his or her neck that says, "Make me feel important." Not only will you succeed in sales, you will succeed in life.

———————

Mary Kay Ash

Light is the task where many share the toil.

———————

Homer

A leader takes people where they want to go.
A great leader takes people where they don't
necessarily want to go, but ought to be.

―――――

Rosalynn Carter

Luck is a matter of preparation
meeting opportunity.

―――――

Oprah Winfrey

Success isn't a result of spontaneous combustion. You must set yourself on fire.

———————

Arnold H. Glasow

The way to gain a good reputation is to endeavor to be what you desire to appear.

———————

Socrates

By embracing risk, you will accomplish more than you ever thought you could. In the process you will transform your life into an exciting adventure that will constantly challenge, reward, and rejuvenate you.

———————

Robert J. Kriegel and Louis Patler

A pat on the back, though only a few vertebrae removed from a kick in the pants, is miles ahead in results.

———

Bennett Cerf

Catch people doing something right! Then tell everyone about it.

———

Kenneth Blanchard

When a man does not know what harbor he is making for, no wind is the right wind.

————————

Lucius Annaeus Seneca

Achievement is largely the product of steadily raising one's level of aspiration and expectation.

———————

Jack Nicklaus

Determine that the thing can and shall be done and then we shall find the way.

———————

Abraham Lincoln

In the long run, men hit only what they aim at.

———————

Henry David Thoreau

Before everything else,

getting ready is the secret of success.

———————

Henry Ford

*I*f you're not learning while you're earning,
you're cheating yourself out of the better
portion of your compensation.

———————

Napoleon Hill

*T*he person who knows how will always have a job.
But the person who knows why will be his boss.

———————

Carl C. Wood

The quality of a man's life is in direct proportion to his commitment to excellence, regardless of his chosen field of endeavor.

———————

Vince Lombardi

A professional is someone who can do his best work when he doesn't feel like it.

———

Alistair Cooke

If hard work is the key to success, most people would rather pick the lock.

———

Claude McDonald

*L*ook at a day when you are
supremely satisfied at the end.
It's not a day when you lounge
around doing nothing.
It's when you've had everything to
do, and you've done it.

———————

Margaret Thatcher

Few things help an individual more than to place responsibility upon him and to let him know that you trust him.

———————

Booker T. Washington

When nobody around you seems to measure up,

it's time to check your yardstick.

———————

Bill Lemley

See everything, overlook a great deal, correct a little.

———————

Pope John XXIII

If there is any secret of success, it lies in the ability to get the other person's point of view and see things from that person's angle as well as your own.

———————

Henry Ford

*Y*our most unhappy customers
are your greatest source of learning.

———————

Bill Gates

*T*he trouble with most of us is
that we would rather be ruined by praise
than saved by criticism.

———————

Norman Vincent Peale

Cooperation is the thorough conviction

that nobody can get there unless

everybody gets there.

———————

Virginia Burden

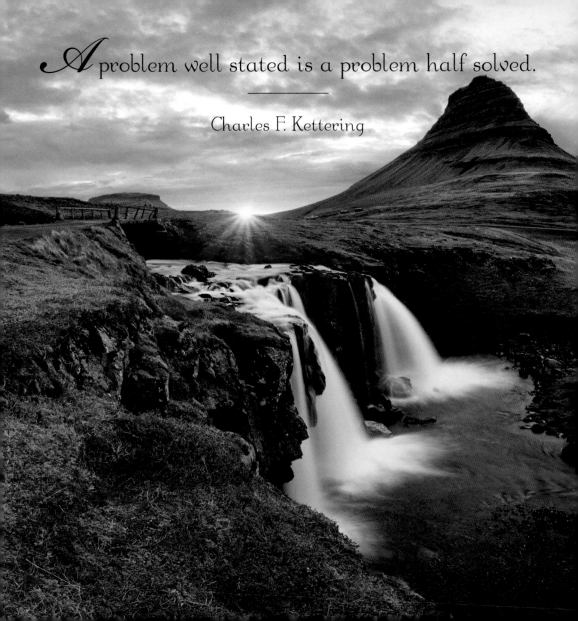

A problem well stated is a problem half solved.

———————

Charles F. Kettering

You don't get harmony when everybody sings the same note.

———————

Doug Floyd

A wise man will make more opportunities than he finds.

———————

Francis Bacon

Let him who would move the world,

first move himself.

———————

Socrates

There is nothing so powerful as an idea

whose time has come.

———————

Victor Hugo

Even if you're on the right track,
you'll get run over if you just sit there.

_____

Will Rogers

The dictionary is the only place where success comes before work.

———————

Vince Lombardi

In making a living today, many no longer leave room for life.

———————

Joseph R. Sizoo

Quotes on Life

Sow a thought, and you reap an action;

Sow an act, and you reap a habit;

Sow a habit, and you reap a character;

Sow a character, and you reap a destiny.

———————

Ralph Waldo Emerson

*T*he greatest discovery of my
generation is that a human being can
alter his life by altering his attitudes.

———————

William James

He that is good for making excuses is
seldom good for anything else.

———

Benjamin Franklin

A man would do nothing if he waited until
he could do it so well that no one could find fault.

———

John Henry Cardinal Newman

Destiny is no matter of chance.

It is a matter of choice.

It is not a thing to be waited for,

it is a thing to be achieved.

———————

William Jennings Bryan

He that will not sail till all dangers

are over must never put to sea.

———————

Thomas Fuller

*I*t is the ability to choose which makes us human.

———————

Madeleine L'Engle

*M*an is not the creature of circumstances.

Circumstances are the creatures of men.

———————

Benjamin Disraeli

You must be the change
you wish to see in the world.

————————

Mahatma Gandhi

Do what you can, with what you have,

where you are.

————————

Theodore Roosevelt

You *ou may be disappointed if you fail,*
but you are doomed if you don't try.

———————

Beverly Sills

You *ou must do the things you think you cannot do.*

———————

Eleanor Roosevelt

Courage is being scared to death—and saddling up anyway.

John Wayne

The greatest use of life is to spend it

for something that will outlast it.

William James

*H*e who has a *why* to live

can bear almost any *how*.

——————

Friedrich Nietzsche

The future belongs to those who believe

in the beauty of their dreams.

———————

Eleanor Roosevelt

Our life is what our thoughts make it.

Marcus Aurelius Antoninus

Give us clear vision, that we may know where to stand and what to stand for—because unless we stand for something, we shall fall for anything.

———————

Peter Marshall

*H*itch your wagon to a star.

———————

Ralph Waldo Emerson

*H*old fast to dreams, for if dreams die,

life is a broken-winged bird that cannot fly.

———————

Langston Hughes

*I*t is good to have an end to journey toward,
but it is the journey that matters in the end.

———

Ernest Hemingway

*T*here is more to life than increasing its speed.

———

Mahatma Gandhi

Life engenders life.

Energy creates energy.

It is by spending oneself that one becomes rich.

———————

Sarah Bernhardt

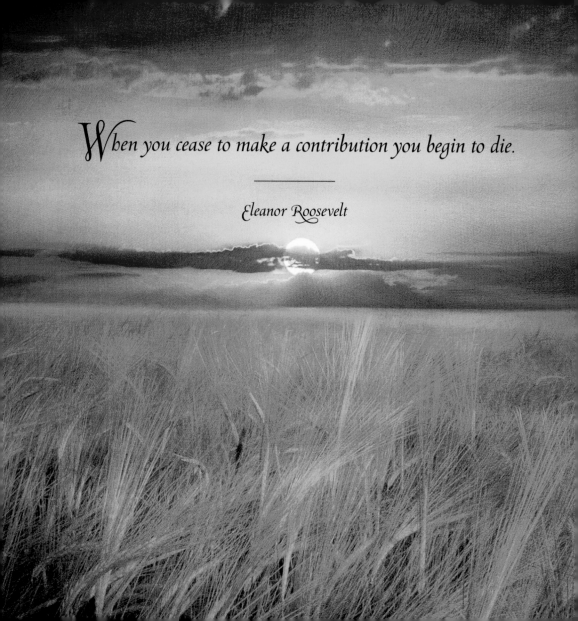

When you cease to make a contribution you begin to die.

——————

Eleanor Roosevelt

At the end of your life, you will never regret not having passed one more test, not winning one more verdict, or not closing one more deal. You will regret time not spent with a husband, a friend, a child, or a parent.

———

Barbara Bush

*L*earn to say no.

It will be of more use to you

than to be able to read Latin.

————————

Charles Haddon Spurgeon

*C*onviction is worthless unless

it is converted into conduct.

————————

Thomas Carlyle

It matters not how a man dies, but how he lives.

———————

Samuel Johnson

No life ever grows great until it is focused, dedicated, and disciplined.

———————

Henry Emerson Fosdick

The expedient thing and the right thing
are seldom the same thing.

―――――

Charles Brower

People who fight fire with fire
usually end up with ashes.

―――――

Abigail Van Buren

*N*o man, for any considerable period,

can wear one face to himself, and another

to the multitude, without finally getting

bewildered as to which may be the true.

————————

Nathaniel Hawthorne

The only way on earth to multiply happiness is to divide it.

———————

Paul Scherer

The only ones among you who will be really happy are those who will have sought and found how to serve.

———————

Albert Schweitzer

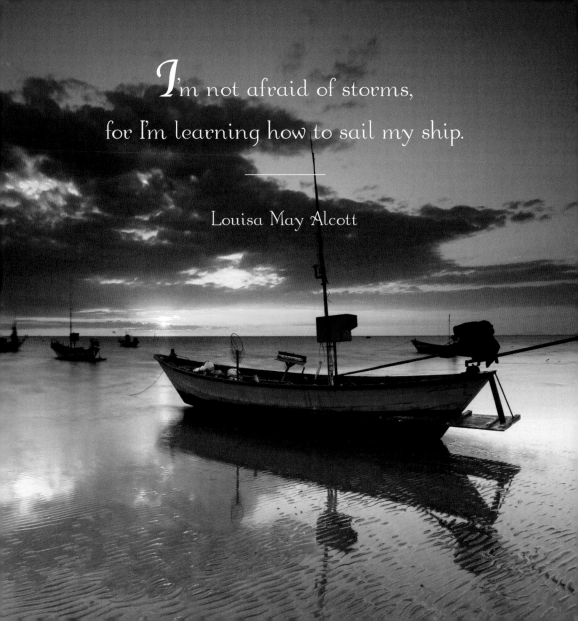

I'm not afraid of storms,

for I'm learning how to sail my ship.

_____

Louisa May Alcott

What do we live for if it is not to make life less difficult for each other?

———————

George Eliot

The unexamined life is not worth living.

———————

Socrates

Man's mind, stretched to a new idea,
never goes back to its original dimensions.

————————

Oliver Wendell Holmes Jr.

Self-development is a higher duty
than self-sacrifice.

————

Elizabeth Cady Stanton

If you haven't any charity in your heart,
you have the worst kind of heart trouble.

————

Bob Hope

We ourselves feel that what we are doing is just a drop in the ocean. But the ocean would be less because of that missing drop.

Mother Teresa

We are not held back by the love we didn't
receive in the past, but by the love we're not
extending in the present.

_____

Marianne Williamson

To ease another's heartache is to forget one's own.

_____

Abraham Lincoln

When it comes to staying young, a mind-lift beats a face-lift any day.

———

Marty Bucella

*L*et no one ever come to you
without leaving better and happier.

————————

Mother Teresa

*G*ood thoughts bear good fruit,
bad thoughts bear bad fruit.

————————

James Allen

What you can do, or dream you can, begin it: Boldness has genius, power, and magic in it.

———————

Johann Wolfgang von Goethe

Do not let what you cannot do interfere with what you can do.

———————

John Wooden

What many of us need most is a good vigorous kick in the seat of the can'ts.

———

Ame Babcock

Until you make peace with who you are, you'll never be content with what you have.

———

Doris Mortman

Character is the sum total of our everyday choices.

———

Margaret Jensen

There is no pillow so soft as a clear conscience.

———

French Proverb

*W*herever we look upon this earth,

the opportunities take shape within the problems.

———

Nelson A. Rockefeller

*N*one are so empty as those who are full of themselves.

————————

*B*enjamin Whichcote

*F*eeling gratitude and not expressing it

is like wrapping a present and not giving it.

————————

*W*illiam *A*rthur *W*ard

Doing your best at this moment

puts you in the best place for the next moment.

———————

Oprah Winfrey

When we put ourselves in the other's place,

we're less likely to want to put him in his place.

———————

Farmer's Digest

*T*here is a time in the life of every problem when
it is big enough to see, yet small enough to solve.

———————

Mike Leavitt

Adversity causes some men to break, others to break records.

William Arthur Ward

Often we change jobs, friends, and spouses instead of ourselves.

Akbarali H. Jetha

When one is out of touch with oneself, one cannot touch others.

————————

Anne Morrow Lindbergh

You can't get ahead while you are getting even.

————————

Dick Armey

How we spend our days is, of course, how we spend our lives.

———

Annie Dillard

*I*f you have made mistakes,

even serious ones,

there is always another chance for you.

What we call failure is not the falling down,

but the staying down.

———————

Mark Pickford

*P*ast experience should be a guide post,

not a hitching post.

———————

D. W. Williams

*U*ltimately, time is all you have

and the idea isn't to save it but to savor it.

———————

Ellan Goodman, *Washington Post*

Time flies, but remember, you're the navigator.

———

St. Louis Bugle

The art of being wise

is the art of knowing what to overlook.

———

William James

Some of us think holding on makes one strong,

but sometimes it's letting go.

Herman Hesse

We are always complaining that our days are few...

and acting as though there would be no end to them.

Lucius Annaeus Seneca

*P*lenty of people miss their share of happiness, not because they never found it but because they didn't stop to enjoy it.

————

William Feather

*T*o be trusted is a greater compliment than being loved.

————

George MacDonald

One of the most tragic things I know about human nature is that all of us tend to put off living. We are all dreaming of some magical rose garden over the horizon—instead of enjoying the roses that are blooming outside our windows today.

———

Dale Carnegie

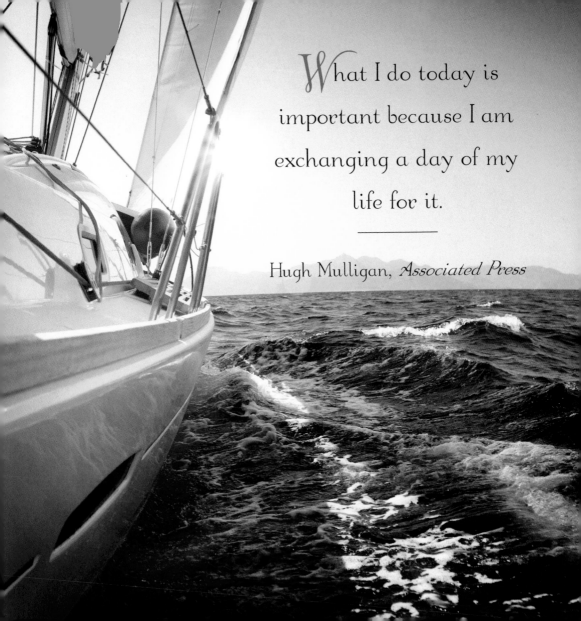

What I do today is important because I am exchanging a day of my life for it.

Hugh Mulligan, *Associated Press*

About the Author

Stephen R. Covey, one of *TIME* magazine's twenty-five most influential Americans, dedicated his life to demonstrating with profound yet straightforward guidance how every person can control his or her destiny. He was an internationally respected leadership authority, family expert, teacher, organizational consultant, and author. He sold over 20 million books (in 40 languages), and *The 7 Habits of Highly Effective People* was named one of the most influential books of the 20th century. His other bestselling books include *Principle-Centered Leadership, First Things First, The 7 Habits of Highly Effective Families, The 8th Habit: From Effectiveness to Greatness*, and *The Leader in Me: How Schools and Parents Around the World Are Inspiring Greatness One Child at a Time*. He was the cofounder of FranklinCovey, a leading global education and training firm with offices in 147 countries.

Dr. Covey was a tenured professor at the Huntsman School of Business, Utah State University, where he held the Jon M. Huntsman Presidential Chair in Leadership. He lived with his wife and family in Utah.

If you have enjoyed this book we invite you to check out our entire collection of gift books, with free inspirational movies, at **www.simpletruths.com.** You'll discover it's a great way to inspire **friends** and **family,** or to thank your best **customers** and **employees.**

For more information, please visit us at:
www.simpletruths.com Or call us toll free… **800-900-3427**